Cobblestone Landmarks of New York State

A York State Book

Cobblestone Landmarks of New York State

OLAF WILLIAM SHELGREN, Jr.
CARY LATTIN
ROBERT W. FRASCH

Photographs by GERDA PETERICH

SYRACUSE UNIVERSITY PRESS   1978

This book is published with the assistance of a grant from the
John Ben Snow Foundation.

Library of Congress Cataloging in Publication Data

Shelgren, Olaf William.
  Cobblestone landmarks of New York State.

  (A York State book)
  1. Cobblestone buildings—New York (State)
2. Vernacular architecture—New York (State)
I. Lattin, Cary, joint author. II. Frasch, Robert W.,
joint author. III. Peterich, Gerda. IV. Title.
NA730.N4S53   721′.0441   78-13994
ISBN 0-8156-2201-5
ISBN 0-8156-0149-2 pbk.

Manufactured in the United States of America

To Gerda Peterich

GERDA PETERICH's photographs are the soul of this book. She was born in Europe, the daughter of Professor Paul Peterich, a sculptor, and Elsbeth Peterich, a pianist. Brought up in an artistic environment, she learned the special qualities of stone while watching her father at work in his studio and on long walks with him through the countryside. Her photographic training was in Germany at the Photografische Lehranstalt, Lette-Verein, Berlin. In 1938 she came to the United States. Eventually, she came to Rochester. For a time she was on the staff of the International Museum of Photography, and in 1957 she received a Master of Fine Arts degree from the University of Rochester. Her thesis for this was on the calotype and its use in architectural photography. While in Rochester she began photographing cobblestone buildings, an activity she continued later on the faculty of Syracuse University. Her death in 1974 prevented her from photographing all the cobblestone buildings originally intended to be included in this book. The bulk of her cobblestone photographs are now in the collection of the Cobblestone Society.

OLAF WILLIAM SHELGREN, JR., is an architect in Buffalo, N.Y. He sits on the Buffalo Landmark and Preservation Board and is a trustee of the Landmark Society of the Niagara Frontier. During his term as president of the Cobblestone Society (1966–74) he brought together these people whose enthusiasm for cobblestone buildings has culminated in this book.

CARY LATTIN, retired Orleans County Historian, is a founder of the Cobblestone Society, an outstanding local historian, a superb raconteur, and lives in a cobblestone house outside of Albion, N.Y.

ROBERT W. FRASCH, historian and educator, is Director of the School of Science and Man at the Rochester Museum and Science Center and was the first president of the Cobblestone Society, 1960–66. He is a member and chairman of the Rochester Preservation Board and past president of the Genesee Country Historical Federation.

CONTENTS

APOLOGIES...

TO THOSE OF YOU WHO LOOK in vain through the following pages for a particular building and do not find it, the authors offer their apologies. Perhaps it is unknown to us; more likely space limitations have prevented its inclusion. But we hope that you will discover at least one building, hitherto unknown to you, as a consolation prize. Surnames of the original owners are used to identify builders where they are known to the authors.

...and ACKNOWLEDGMENTS

WESTERN NEW YORKERS have always taken cobblestone buildings more or less for granted. Carl Schmidt of Scottsville was one of the first persons to take them seriously. His two books on the subject did much to make people aware of the uniqueness of western New York's cobblestone buildings. When destruction threatened the cobblestone church building on the Ridge Road (Rt. 104) in the hamlet of Childs, Gaines township, Orleans County, the Cobblestone Society was born. After this landmark was saved several members of the Society realized that a pictorial survey of cobblestone buildings would be welcome. The New York State Council on the Arts agreed and generously funded its preparation.

Books of this sort come about with the help of many people. Mr. & Mrs. Lawrence W. Gracey of Geneva, Mrs. Dorothy S. Facer of Lyons, and Clyde Maffin of Canandaigua have all been most generous with their time in helping locate and research buildings and assisting on photography expeditions. Others who have helped are Marjorie Allen, Anna E. Patchett, Mrs. C. E. Conner, Mrs. Bernard E. Harkness, John Genung, Elizabeth Holahan, and Mrs. Virginia Barons. Lilly E. Hoffmann and M. J. Gladstone have been most supportive during the long period of preparation. Finally, Evelyn Lyman and Francis R. Kowsky have given the text a polishing, and Helen J. Robinson provided the manuscript typing. The authors gratefully acknowledge all this help.

Buffalo, N.Y.   OWS, Jr.
Fall 1978   CL
                                                                            RWF

x

Cobblestone Landmarks of New York State

THE STONES AND THE STYLE

OUR UPSTATE COBBLESTONE LANDMARKS are works of art created by pioneer craftsmen in the middle third of the nineteenth century. Using an Ice Age residue of glacially rounded native stones, those craftsmen of the 1830s and 1840s perfected a form of folk art that was without precedent in America. For approximately thirty years they created a variety of decorative walls on hundreds of buildings. Today their creations are unique among all those structures erected in the Great Lakes region before the Industrial Revolution rendered such craftsmanship economically obsolete.

The evolution of the humble cobblestone began 325–475 million years ago. During the Ordovician, Silurian, and Devonian periods of the Paleozoic Era all of the Great Lakes region west of the present Hudson Valley was a great shallow salt sea filled with living creatures whose remains, falling to the bottom, gradually formed layers of limestone deposits. Erosion of the young Appalachian Mountains, a more ancient land mass to the east of this salty sea, washed down additional layers of sand and clay, depositing these in thicknesses of thousands of feet. Under enormous pressure, these various layers of sediment became limestone, dolomite, sandstone, and shale. Finally, some 250 million years ago, as the salty, sediment-filled sea dried up and the land mass emerged, new rivers began to cut into and expose our regional sedimentary bedrock. The forces of erosion, pressure, and time that produced this foundation were eventually to form the cobbles * that later were wrought from this same bedrock.

---

* Geologists classify stones by size as follow: pebble, 4–64 mm., .16″–2.5″; cobblestone, 64–256 mm., 2.5″–10.1″; boulder, over 256 mm., over 10.1″. In lay terms a pebble is a stone held by two fingers, a cobblestone is that held by one hand, and a boulder needs two hands to hold.

1

In the last million years or so the Ice Age redesigned our landscape. Great juggernaut masses of ice ground loose stones on top of the bedrock surface into a generous supply of cobblestones, smoothing the bedrock surface as well. Advancing slowly down from Labrador, these glaciers and ice sheets picked up rock rubble and carried it south. Thus, in addition to polishing and redistributing the loose fragments of local sedimentary sandstone and limestone, the ice mass brought with it a small number of harder Canadian metamorphic stones, such as gneiss and quartzite, which were tumbled and crushed along the way. These stones were eventually left on the land when the ice melted. Geologists call this glacial deposit of rocky debris over the bedrock layer the till sheet or drift mantle. The layman knows it as topsoil or subsoil.

There are two types of till or drift deposits: ice-laid and water-laid. Stones from an ice-laid deposit are roughly rounded fragments of many sizes and kinds of rock. These are what have come to be called field cobbles; perhaps more properly they should be called glaciated cobbles. The glaciated cobbles are found predominately in the drumlin areas of central and western New York, between Rochester and Syracuse. In contrast, stones from water-laid deposits have had their sharp edges rounded and their surfaces smoothed. These are the stones that were released from the ice and then subjected to additional tumbling action in glacial-born waters of streams and lakes. These water-rounded cobbles are found predominately in the moraine areas of central and western New York. Lake Ontario's present shoreline for the most part is lined with water-rounded stones, and here wave action continues the process of cobblestone polishing. Thus, through the advent of natural forces a natural building material was deposited and shaped in central and western New York.

Following the American Revolution, settlers began to push, and be pushed, westward into new lands in central and western New York. Initially, surviving and conquering the forested land were their immediate concerns. Forests had to be cleared to provide farm lands on which food crops might be planted. The houses they built first on their new lands were usually log or hand-hewn frame cabins, although virgin hardwood forests of maple, beech, and oak did not surrender easily to the farmer's axe. To the first generation of farmers the axe, broadaxe, froe, saw, and other woodworking tools were no less important than the plow. With these tools the farmer began many years of forest removal and with them put up his rude log or frame cabin in the forest clearing. Sawmills, gristmills, and other water-powered mills were rapidly constructed wherever streams could be damned. Locally milled lumber was a necessary luxury when increasing numbers of farm buildings were needed for a completely self-sufficient farm economy.

The farmer's remaining woodlots of uncleared land supplied fuel and free construction materials for the growing farm complex. With a broadaxe, felled trees were squared into massive beams and then pegged together to form the skeletons of barns, animal shelters, stables, carriage sheds, woodsheds, granaries, and other farm buildings. Split logs and fieldstones became fences. Lumber for walls and floors was cut at the closest sawmill. Hand-split wooden shingles made excellent roofs and siding. As the necessities of life were secured, larger frame houses replaced log cabins to accommodate growing families. Between 1800 and 1820 brickyards, stone quarries, lime kilns, and glass factories appeared in every corner of the state to offer farmers and townfolk alike a choice between wood, brick, or stone construction.

In central and western New York settling the land proceeded slowly, due mainly to the scarcity of natural transportation routes. Waterways were the simplest mode of transportation, and west of the Mohawk River there was scarcely anything of this sort. In 1817, following an unsuccessful attempt to have the federal government build an artificial waterway to the West, New York State started the project on its own. Derisively called "Clinton's

Ditch" by its opponents (in honor of the governor and principal proponent), the Erie Canal began to thread its way westward toward Lake Erie. The canal required construction workers with various skills, among them masons to quarry and lay stone for canal locks and aqueducts. To build these the remnant of the prehistoric sea—limestone—was quarried for stone blocks. Quarried limestone was also crushed and burned to produce lime for the mortar with which these blocks were laid. The canal provided the first opportunity for subsistence farmers to become cash crop farmers, for their crops could now be carried back east to established centers of population. In 1825 the canal was finally connected with Lake Erie, linking the Great Lakes with the Atlantic Ocean via waterways across New York State. From New England more Yankee farmers came to take up lands in western New York. Financial prosperity came with the marketing of their wheat, flour, and other cash crops on the Atlantic seaboard.

The newly prosperous farmers were now able to build houses reflecting this prosperity and their confidence in the future. Building materials in those days usually came from the immediate area, and only in rare instances were they transported great distances, as is common now. Central and western New York had, in addition to timber and clay for bricks, all the stones, gravel, and sand left by the glaciers of long ago. Sometime after 1825 the first cobblestone building was constructed in upstate New York, probably in Wayne or Monroe County, and the cobblestone era was begun. We do not know which building was the first, where it was, or who the mason was. In the years to come virtually every type of building was constructed in this regional mode, incorporating within them most of the popular architectural styles of the early nineteenth century. The majority of cobblestone buildings are in the Greek Revival style, which appeared in western New York about 1835. Those constructed before this date are in the Federal style. Gothic Revival and Italianate style cobblestone buildings are relatively few.

While most of the cobblestone structures built were farmhouses, since most upstate New Yorkers were farmers, cobblestone structures were built in villages and cities also, including a business block in Batavia, a reaper manufacturing building in Perry, a warehouse in Palmyra, and an agricultural equipment factory in Macedon, all razed years ago.

In all more than 700 cobblestone buildings were built in the counties to the south of Lake Ontario. Most are concentrated on the Lake Ontario Plain and among the Finger Lakes, but some isolated examples were built as far south as Bath, Elmira, and Cortland. Wayne County exceeds all others with over 150 documented buildings. Monroe, Orleans, and Ontario counties each record about 100 buildings. There is even a cobblestone house in Colorado, built by a Monroe County man who went west after the Civil War.

Following the frontier, New Yorkers soon carried the craft west to new farms and villages in southern Ontario, Canada, southern Michigan, and beyond Lake Michigan as far as Beloit, Wisconsin. Chester Clark of Marion, N.Y., whose 1838 letters to *The Genesee Farmer and Gardener's Journal* provide us with an early document of the art, and his brothers introduced cobblestone masonry in 1844 to Beloit, where they built the Smith-Gaston house and several more prior to 1863. Levi Boughton learned the cobblestone craft in Monroe County and took it to Paris, Ontario, Canada, in 1838. There twelve houses and two churches were built.

Thus, on both sides of the Illinois-Wisconsin border the second largest group of American cobblestone buildings appeared in the 1840s and 1850s. In fact, much of the best cobblestone work in Wisconsin and southern Michigan is located in or near places with transplanted New York names such as Rochester, Geneva, Troy, Farmington, Palmyra, Genesee, and Walworth.*

A much less significant number of cobblestone structures is found

* See Richard W. E. Perrin, *Wisconsin Magazine of History* 47(2)(Winter 1963–64).

scattered in a thin line eastward through the Mohawk Valley to Guilderland in Albany County, and Bennington and Brattleboro, Vermont. Eight hundred and fifty miles and almost as many cobblestone buildings separate Brattleboro from Beloit, but the dates clearly indicate that the idea moved west and east from its origin in upstate New York.

HISTORICAL ANTECEDENTS

COBBLESTONE MASONRY may have come to western New York from England, for English masons helped build the stoneworks for the Erie Canal. But this connection is conjectural, and perhaps it can never be proven. In southeastern England—in and around Brighton, Worthing, Rottingdean, and Ovingdean—beginning about 1790 a number of structures were built of beach flints (local water-rounded cobbles) laid in straight rows with the horizontal mortar joints troweled to a flat projecting V. Further north in England, near Sherringham, Norfolk, is another group of beach flint buildings, constructed about the same time, but without any special emphasis of the horizontal mortar joints. *Flint* is used in England to describe construction using the flint stone.

The English technique of constructing buildings of flints has a long tradition. One historian even credits its origin to the Saxons. It is also possible that the Saxons learned the technique from the Romans since there are third-century Roman fortifications erected to protect the south and east coasts against Saxon invaders. Flint construction continued through the Middle Ages and the Gothic era in southeastern England and East Anglia. The flints were laid sometimes in straight rows and sometimes in random uncoursed patterns without any special emphasis on the mortar joints (before c. 1790). Corners were built up using cut stone or brick, where cut stone was not readily available. Flints were also combined with brick and cut stone to make patterned walls.* In the sixteenth century walls faced with knapped (split) flints made their appearance.

* See J. Charles Cox, *The English Parish Church* (1914); Alec Clifton-Taylor, *The Pattern of English Building* (London: Faber & Faber, 1972); and P. H. Ditchfield, *The Charm of the English Village* (1908).

LEWES, SUSSEX, ENGLAND, #19 Sun Street

Here in Lewes, Sussex, England, an ancient inland town with the impressive remains of a once mighty castle, we find an early nineteenth-century town house with a façade of coursed beach flints and painted brick details. It is the only cobble structure on Sun Street in a town with but few cobble buildings. In Sussex, as in New York State, cobblestone structures are a minority. Photograph by Robert W. Frasch.

Shoreham-by-Sea, Sussex, England, Manor House, Church Street

Shoreham-by-Sea is well known for its two well-preserved Norman churches, with St. Mary's de Haura being especially impressive. This Manor House at the head of Church Street stands just outside of that churchyard and is one of a group of late eighteenth-century flint buildings, nearly all of coursed beach flint with two of knapped (split) flint. These include numbers 9, 11, 18, 20, 22, 24, all clustered on a short street between the churchyard and the main thoroughfare. One house with coursed beach flint, #20, bears a 1754 datestone. This entire block is re-emerging as a historic district because of local preservation efforts encouraged by Great Britain's Town and Country Planning Act. Photograph by Robert W. Frasch.

West Tarring, Sussex, England, 54–56 Church Road, Detail
A prototype for New York State's typical cobblestone masonry mortar treatment is found on this double house just a few miles inland from Sussex beaches. Coursed beach flints are used with mortar shaped into raised triangles between each stone and into a raised ridge between rows of stones. Photograph by Robert W. Frasch.

Ovingdean, Sussex, England, St. Wulfram's Church Rectory, Detail, 1804–1807

Along the English Channel coast of Sussex, England, rounded beach flints were used for building construction in a manner identical in every respect to American cobblestone masonry construction. This detail of the rectory at St. Wulfram's Church in Ovingdean, Sussex, was constructed 1804–1807 with labor provided by French prisoners of war. The beach flints are laid in neat rows separated by horizontal pyramids added between the stones. The brick quoins are typically English. Like many similar examples in the vicinity of Brighton, this flint cobble structure predates its American cobblestone cousins. Photograph by Robert W. Frasch.

The Normans, who conquered England in 1066, also utilized cobblestones in walls. Carl Schmidt, in *Cobblestone Masonry* (Scottsville, N.Y.: Schmidt, 1966), cites examples of this in and around Dieppe. The French provinces of Dauphiny, Béarn, Burgundy, Roussillon, and the Hautes Pyrénées also have cobblestone buildings.

All across northern Italy, but especially in Lombardy, there are a number of Romanesque and Gothic churches dating from the ninth to the fourteenth centuries whose walls incorporate cobblestones. Occasionally decorated with herringbone patterns, these medieval buildings trace their origins to the Romans, the inventors of concrete, who perfected the construction of rubble stone walls.* Wherever the Romans built they adapted their methods to the materials available locally. In the shallow rivers of northern Italy they found a copious supply of "river pebbles" which they employed as a filler in the standard forms of Lombard wall construction. Ancient techniques apparently survived into and beyond the Middle Ages in vernacular architecture. In the sixteenth century, Palladio, the greatest architect of the Italian Renaissance and a man who was aware of both local tradition and ancient practice, built low cobblestone walls to line the broad approach roads to the Villa Barbaro (1560) at Maser, near Vicenza. For later generations, Palladio's use of cobblestone bestowed the mantle of respectability upon this age-old building material.

* Arthur Kingsley Porter, *Lombard Architecture* (1915); G. R. Rivoira, *Roman Architecture and its Principles of Construction under the Empire* (Oxford: Clarendon Press, 1925).

VERONA, ITALY, Duomo, Detail of cloister wall, 12th century
In this wall rows of cobblestones are laid in a herringbone pattern. The alternating bands of cobblestones and cut stone or brick are a continuation of the ancient Roman method for constructing a rubble wall. Photograph by Francis R. Kowsky.

MASONRY CONSTRUCTION

COBBLESTONE MASONRY is a folk art. It was primitive at first and highly refined toward the end of its short life in upstate New York. Some of the masons' names are known, as Carl Schmidt reports; most are anonymous. Little can be inferred from the few known names that could not be "read" in the buildings themselves. Only a few masons built more than three or four houses. hardly enough for the lifelong sustenance of a trained craftsman. Obviously, these masons also worked in brick and quarried stone and were not solely cobblestone masonry specialists. They learned the cobblestone technique from each other or by examining finished buildings and relied on the age-old method of rubble wall construction for most of their buildings.

Three basic types of cobblestone wall construction were employed in New York. The earliest walls were laid up with a complete integration of the exterior cobblestone surface and the inner wall. Here, just as in early Roman rubble walls, the exterior layer cannot be distinguished from the interior structure. The entire thickness of the wall is laid up in one operation, a most durable form of construction. With the gradual refinement of exterior textures a second type of construction came into being: a facing of cobbles, usually the water-rounded variety, is laid up with extra-long stones reaching into the rubble core to bond the facing to the core. The facing stones are of varying lengths, but the exposed exterior faces match each other in shape and size. The outer surface was laid up along with the backing wall. This, too, is durable construction. The third method is the least permanent: a rubble wall is laid up first, after which a decorative cobblestone and mortar veneer is added separately. Cobbles are small, and there are no bonding stones. Buildings which show the finest wall textures are usually built by this method

A ruined wall in the Mendon area illustrates the earliest and simplest type of cobblestone wall construction, a complete integration of the exterior surface and inner wall.

A ruined wall in the Webster area shows a second, more refined type of construction, in which extra-long cobblestones secure the outer surface to the rubble core of the wall.

which unfortunately is prone to damage from the elements (Plate 87). When cracks occur in the veneer due to irregular settling of the wall, water penetrates them and frost wedging results, detaching the veneer from the rubble core. Repairs of such damage can usually be detected by the different color of the mortar. Portland cement, commonly used in mortar today, has a blue-gray color and is darker than the warm-colored mortars used in pre–Civil War buildings.*

Contemporary accounts describe cobblestone building construction. *The Genesee Farmer & Gardener's Journal,* published by Luther Tucker at Rochester, New York, carried in the January 1838 issue an inquiry about cobblestone walls. The anonymous inquirer suggested a more extensive use of cobblestones "for their extreme plenty here, would render them far cheaper than brick or flat stone. . . . The stone must be picked up at all event, and we might as well put them together for a building. . . . But will these walls stand . . . and if so, how are they constructed?" The answer, a description of a steam flouring mill (now demolished) in the Wayne County village of Palmyra, came in the March issue of the same year from Chester Clark of Marion, Wayne County:

I cheerfully transmit a few facts. . . . Having erected two or three buildings each season, for several years past, I shall only mention one which I built last season. It is 40 x 60, four stories high. The foundation is three feet high, the first story $10\frac{8}{12}$, . . . making from the foundation to the plate $48\frac{4}{12}$ feet in height, with a wing 24 feet by 34, one story. The whole was built of cobblestone (not of first quality). The outside was laid in courses of cobblestone four inches in thickness, and larger stone on the inside. . . . As regards the durability, I am perfectly convinced that if they are laid with good materials,

* See Edward Shaw, *Operative Masonry: Or, a Theoretical and Practical Treatise of Building* (1832).

The most fragile type of cobblestone masonry was used on this side wall in Yates County. Although it is the most decorative method of construction, the cobblestone veneer is prone to damage, especially cracks and frost wedging.

they will stand and their solidarity increases as their age increases. The quality of sand with the lime is very essential. The coarser and purer the sand, the stronger will be the cement and the firmer the wall. As for the proper quantity of sand with the lime, it depends on the coarseness and the purity. The proportion which I generally use, is from five to eight bushels of sand to one of lime in the stone.

"Lime in the stone" probably refers to limestone after burning, but before grinding or pulverizing. Limestone changes its weight but not its volume in burning.

P. S. Bonsteel (the name is now spelled Bonesteele) in a letter to *The Cultivator* 9 (7) (1842), another rural journal, furnishes some information about the thickness of the walls of his house which he built in 1835: "my plan for thickness of wall was, the cellar wall 20 inches thick to first floor, drop off two inches to second floor, then drop off two inches and extend out to top . . . Sort your stones so as to have the outside courses 3 or 4 inches, with straight lines for cement. Take the coarsest of sand. . . . I used the common stone lime, one bushel to seven of sand."

Another letter to *The Cultivator* 8(3)(1841), from Cayuga County describes a different method of construction:

Cobblestones of any size not exceeding six inches in diameter may be used, but for the regular courses on the outside those of two inches in diameter should be preferred. Small stones give the building a much neater aspect. Two inch stones are very neat, though three inch stones will answer. The inside row of stones may be twice as large as those on the outside. . . . Mortar . . . eight to nine bushels of clean, sharp sand to one bushel of fresh stone lime . . . the strength of the building depends on the goodness of the mortar . . . The thickness of the wall is sixteen inches, though twelve inches will answer very well for the gable ends above the garret floor . . . When the foundation, or cellar wall is leveled and prepared, a layer of two (or two and a half) inches of mortar is spread over it, and the stones are laid down into the mortar in two rows which mark the outside and the inside of the wall leaving about an inch between each adjoining stone in the same row. If the wall is to be grouted [mortar, sufficiently fluid, poured between the stones filling the interstices] the two rows are formed into two ridges by filling the vacancies between the stones with mortar, and the space between these ridges (about a foot in width) is filled with such stones as are not wanted for the regular courses. The grout is then applied. If the wall is not to be grouted however, the mortar should be carefully pressed around every stone, making the wall solid without flaw or interstice. When one course is levelled, begin another. P. S. Since writing the above, I have received two communications. . . . One says "the thickness of the wall is measured from the outside of the stones. Pieces of timber, four to six inches and two feet long, are used in setting the lines. These are laid in the course just finished, and the line is drawn through saw cuts just 16 inches apart."

This is the Roman technique of infilling the rubble with mortar. Unfortunately, there are no written accounts of the use of planks to keep the wall plumb and the rows in the veneer straight. But oral testimony of the use of planks has come down to us, and an investigation of walls reveals that certain patterns could hardly have been created without such a device. The method has been employed since Roman times. We find a description of it by H. G. Richey in his book, *The Building Mechanic's Ready Reference* (1907): "To keep those stones straight and in line until the mortar hardens is a very difficult piece of work for the mason. A quick and easy method is to build a form of plank for the face of the wall . . . and build the cobblestones up against this form. This will make a straight and even wall, such as can be obtained in no other way. After the mortar has hardened, the form can be taken down and the joints between the cobblestones cleaned out and pointed."

It has been discovered in several cobblestone houses, when new openings were cut through old walls, that there existed an air space from two to three inches thick for the full height of the wall. This "cavity wall" was intended to insulate the house.

Today we are easily confused by the variety of builders' formulas for the mortar mix of their cobblestone masonry. This is because we have become almost completely dependent on Portland cement since the 1880s. Portland cement is a patented formula for an exceptionally strong and unyielding, waterproof cement. It assures a highly standardized product of uniform consistency, more suitable to modern types of construction.

Cobblestone masons were describing an entirely different product. Their lime-sand mortars (not cement) have been in common use for centuries. In contrast to Portland cement, lime mortar was comparatively soft, slower to set, more flexible, and of more varied consistency. Much depended on the quality of the limestone, sand, and water locally available. Limestone obtained from different locations had different chemical components. Likewise, sand deposits might contain sharp or rounded granules mixed with varying amounts of organic material. Knowing the qualities of their local lime and sand resources, masons combined experience with skill to vary the proportions needed for a durable mortar.

Much experimentation with mortars took place during the building of the Erie Canal by engineers who were troubled by the problem of common lime mortar not being stable under water. Hydraulic mortar (i.e., mortar which will set under water) was needed, but the well-known European hydraulic cements were too expensive to import. During canal excavations in Chittenango natural cement rock (a type of limestone called waterlime) was discovered reaching from Port Jervis through Oneida, Auburn, Geneva, and Batavia, to Buffalo. Natural cement yields a mortar which will not only set under water, but sets much quicker and becomes stronger in air than common lime cement. Its color is the buff most common in cobblestone walls.*

Limestone outcroppings were also readily accessible throughout the Great Lakes region. Large quantities of limestone fragments, or lime rock, together with large quantities of firewood were stacked into hillside lime kilns and burned to 1,650°F for nearly two days. After carbon dioxide was given off, the lumps remaining became calcium oxide or quicklime. It was essential for this quicklime to be kept free from moisture until ready for use. For any long-term storage or shipping it was put in tightly sealed wooden barrels.

The transformation of quicklime into lime required pulverizing and slaking. Slaking is the addition of water, and several methods for this were used. Perhaps the most common was to prepare a protected pit at the construction site and in it mix pulverized quicklime and water, making a paste. The slaking lime gave off heat and expanded in volume before it was ready for use as a clear white paste. The color of the mortar largely depended on the color of the sand that was added.†

---

* See Harley J. McKee, "Canvas White and Natural Cement, 1818–1834," *Journal of the Society of Architectural Historians* 20(4).

† Caution is urged when repointing or repairing original softer lime mortar with modern harder cements. The color of the repair mortar rarely matches the old mortar, making an obvious scar. In extreme cases irreparable damage can result due to basic differences between lime mortar and Portland cement mortar. Repairs should match older mortar in color, texture, strength, and hardness. Lime mortars are still available, and they can be mixed with cements. Tints are also available to approximate original colors. The best advice yet given is to begin repairs at the rear of a building so experience can guide more successful repairs on the front. An outstanding guide is Harley J. McKee *Introduction to Early American Masonry, Stone, Brick, Mortar and Plaster*, Columbia University Series on the Technology of Early American Buildings (Washington D.C.: National Trust for Historic Preservation, 1973). A detailed discussion of mortar is presented in the *Bulletin of the Association for Preservation Technology* APT 6(1) (1974).

Once mixed, the lime mortar remained plastic for only a few hours before it set and could support the weight of succeeding layers of stone. Hardening, in contrast to modern cements, took place at a slow rate over months and even years before the final strength was achieved. This slow rate of hardening gave the new building time to settle and adjust to the site without cracks appearing.

Of equal importance as the foregoing methods of wall construction are the treatments of door and window openings, and corners. Here we find the use of wood, fieldstone, cut stone, and brick. Lintels over doors and windows were most often cut stone, infrequently brick. In a few instances the lintel is a jack or flat arch of roughly squared fieldstones. Window sills are of wood or cut stone. The corners of the buildings are, for the most part, formed with cut stone quoins, but we also find corners with brick quoins, wood pilasters, roughly cut stone piers, and even a few rounded cobblestone corners. The following advertisement appeared in the *Rochester Republican* of June 16, 1837:

> Smith Stone Quarry: The subscriber can furnish at the Smith Stone quarry on the direct road leading from Rochester to Lima 1 mile and ½ west of the village of Mendon, almost all kinds of building stone, of the best quality; step stones of all shapes and sizes; columns and pillars for open fronts; all kinds of stone used in brick and cobblestone building; door and window caps; sills and thresholds; circle door and window caps; . . . all kind of stone cut to order in plain molding. . . . All communications and orders by mail will be promptly attended to.
>
> G. M. and D. M. Tinker
> West Mendon, December 9, 1836

Cobblestone masonry is mentioned in only one of the builders' handbooks of the pre–Civil War era—*The Economic Cottage Builder* (1855) by Charles P. Dwyer. This book dates toward the end of the great era of cobblestone masonry. Dwyer apparently had little real knowledge of cobblestone masonry, since he said that the cobblestones of the outside veneer were simply hammered into a coat of mortar, or it may have been that the traditional techniques were already being replaced with cheaper, more rapid techniques.

TEXTURE AND PATTERN

THE MOST DISTINCTIVE FEATURE of cobblestone buildings is their texture. Texture is determined by the size and composition of the cobblestones, by the mortar joint treatment, and by the patterns created by mortar joints and cobblestones.

Most cobblestone buildings have smaller stones used on the front and larger stones on the sides and rear. This can be immediately seen when the number of cobblestone courses in height is counted at the stone quoins. This "sizing" results in a finer-grained texture on the front. Oral traditions persist of devices used to grade the cobbles for size. One method employed a board with several holes of different diameters, another, iron rings of different diameters. To date no original device of either kind has come to light.

Closer inspection of the cobblestone wall will reveal an added dimension of artwork expressed in the mortar between the rows of stones. This presented the mason with the opportunity for an even greater variety of artistic expression. The treatment of the mortar joints is three dimensional in New York's cobblestone buildings, with few exceptions. Since the cobbles are laid in horizontal courses, the horizontal mortar joint is usually in the shape of a projecting V, with the point of the V forming a continuous horizontal line between courses (Plate 4). Occasionally this horizontal joint has been finished with a beading trowel, which makes a continuous bead or half-round projection (Plate 22). This continuous line, whether V'd or beaded, provides the horizontal emphasis which helps to bring order to what otherwise could be a random collection of stones. The vertical mortar joints are also finished off, sometimes V-shaped, sometimes into elongated flat pyramids. Only rarely was the mortar left flat. In Webster, Monroe County, how-

ever, one house has the cobbles projecting from an essentially flat mortar surface (Plate 2). This flat surface has been scored with a beading trowel to
provide the continuous horizontal bead between courses and short diagonal
beads in the vertical joints. A mortar joint pattern seen infrequently is one
where horizontal and vertical joints are given equal emphasis with the result
being a honeycomb pattern with a stone nestled into each cell (Plate 31).

The desire for ornamentation led builders to exploit the inherent
character of the stones in various ways. The shapes and colors of the indi-
vidual glaciated or field cobbles made it more difficult for the mason to work
in any patterns other than what could be accomplished with mortar joint
treatment. A rare example of a pattern rendered with glaciated cobbles is
the herringbone, achieved by laying the stones diagonally and reversing the
direction in each successive row (Plate 15). Examples of this type of treatment occur in only a few buildings in Ontario and Yates counties.

The water-rounded cobble gave rise to a greater number of decorative
devices; due to their greater uniformity of size, shape, and color. The herringbone pattern, formed with rather thin oval stones, is found in Orleans,
northern Monroe, Wayne, and northern Ontario counties. This pattern usually forms the entire wall surface of at least one façade (Plate 26). In a few
instances it is found confined to several horizontal courses or the top of the
gable end. The same shape stone—thin oval—has been set vertically in several buildings in Orleans and Niagara counties (Plate 22).   They have also
been used in one house as a single course set immediately above a roughly
cut stone course to mark the first floor line. Oval stones laid horizontally ap-
pear in several buildings in northeastern Orleans and northwestern Monroe
counties. In the Blodget house, Murray Township, Orleans County, every
fourth course of cobbles is composed of horizontal ovals stones (Plate 18).

Color was used to achieve special effects through the careful collection and sorting of water-rounded stones. In Yates, Wayne, Ontario, and

Monroe counties there are a number of buildings whose surfaces are composed exclusively of dark red sandstone cobbles. These cobbles were all apparently originally gathered from Lake Ontario's shoreline in the vicinity of Sodus. The dark red color can deceive the viewer at a distance into assuming that the building is constructed of brick. At Elbridge, Onondaga County, the Gothic style of the Munro house is enhanced by the gray of the cobbles which came from the Oswego area of Lake Ontario (Plates 88 and 89). Parti-color effects are obtained by the selective use of dark red and very light tan or gray cobbles on the fronts of several buildings in Wayne County. At Sodus there is a house whose dark red face is lined at every sixth course with a row of almost white stones. In nearby Wolcott another house is striped, two rows of dark red cobbles alternating with two rows of light brown cobbles.

The beauty of cobblestone buildings depends on light. Without this, particularly sunlight, the texture of the stones and mortar joints are minimized, and the fascinating patterns recede. Sunlight, raking across the textured surface, gives a vibrancy to the building that is unique. Perhaps the most harmonious manifestation of man and nature in upstate New York is the rural cobblestone building dappled by sunlight and surrounded by open fields.

LAKE ONTARIO PLAIN, EAST

Wayne and Northeastern Monroe Counties

Lake Ontario

GENESEE R.

IRONDEQUOIT
BAY

Pultneyville

104

Sodus

SOD
BAY

Webster

Onturio

Williamson

Alton

Ro

250

350

21

88

Rochester

441

Marion

14

Penfield

W A Y N

East
Rochester

31 F

C A N A L

Lyons

31

MONROE

Fair-
port

31

Palmyra

Newark

Allo

ONTARIO

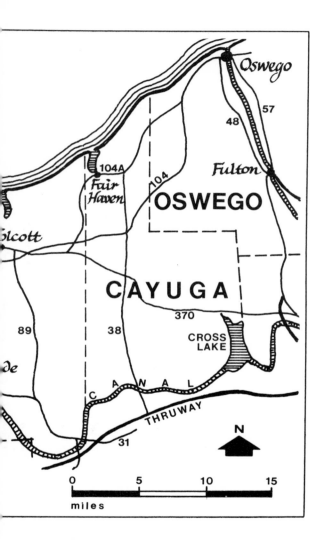

1. Monroe County, Webster Baptist Church, 39 South Avenue, Webster

Construction of the church began in 1855 and was completed in 1857. The entrance, in the stucco-covered lower portion, is a minor feature. The open cupola, with its eight Ionic columns supporting the dome, is the major feature of interest. Its initial function was twofold—to identify the building as a public one and to shelter a bell. The water-rounded cobbles of the front wall are dark red and very small, while the rest of the walls are faced with cobbles of various colors. Stained glass of early twentieth-century origin fills the window openings. This is the largest cobblestone church building of approximately twenty such buildings.

2. Monroe County, House, 93 Main Street, Webster

Brick is used in this house for the quoins and lintels, a detail more frequently encountered in English flint buildings. The field cobbles are quite large and have relatively flat faces. Rather than emphasizing the joints by projecting them in the usual V shape, the mason kept them flat and scored them with a recessed V. The two original chimneys are brick also, as is always the case in cobblestone buildings. The house was built c. 1830. Like many other cobblestone structures built along the northern side of Ridge Road, the rear side has a walkout basement, and the main entrance faces the crest of the natural highway. This sandy ridge marks the shoreline of an Ice Age predecessor of Lake Ontario, which extends from Sodus westward all the way to Toronto, Canada.

3. WAYNE COUNTY, Bigsby House, Lake Road, Ontario Township

The red water-rounded cobbled walls are outlined with white Greek Revival cornices and corner pilasters made of wood instead of the usual stone quoins. The low foundation is faced with roughly cut sandstone. This house dates from the mid-1840s.

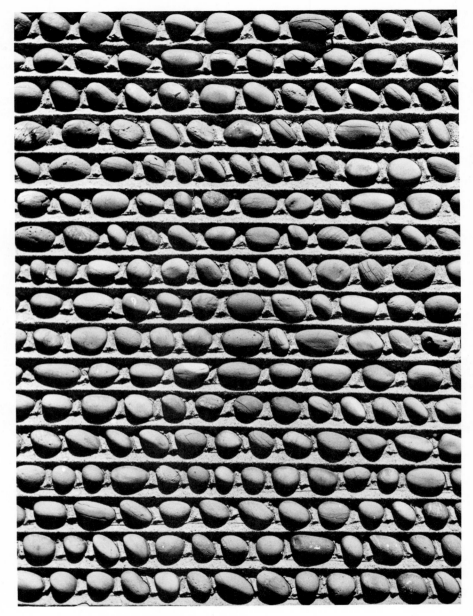

4. WAYNE COUNTY, Bigsby House, Detail

5. WAYNE COUNTY, Waters House, Lake Road, Williamson Township

Zimri Waters' account book covering the years 1844–69 lists Philip Wemesfelder as mason and Rufus Moses as carpenter of his house. The shell of the house was built in 1850, and the interior finished in 1851 and 1852. The construction cost was $350, cash plus farm produce. Moses made the blinds in 1855. The porch on the left wing is original, whereas the porch on the main portion is a twentieth century addition. The frieze windows contain their original cast iron grilles. The cobbles are selected water-rounded red sandstones from the Sodus area.

6. WAYNE COUNTY, Preston House, Lake Road, Sodus Township

William Swales built this house as a wedding gift for his daughter, Elizabeth, and her husband, John Preston, about 1840. It sits on a knoll with its back to Lake Ontario. The window lintels are tapered sandstones forming a flat arch, and the cobbles are water-rounded, predominately red in color with a sprinkling of gray and black. The cornice is Federal in character, while the porch is a handsome addition of the 1870s. Later owners have added a large addition on the right since this picture was taken. A cobblestone barn sits at a discreet distance behind the house and was built at about the same time.

7. WAYNE COUNTY, Martin Harris Farm, Maple Avenue, Palmyra Township
This house was built in 1849 for William Chapman, but it bears the name of the man who owned the land in the 1820s—Martin Harris. He became interested in the Church of the Latter Day Saints. Joseph Smith, founder of this church, dug a well on the property. Harris' interest grew to the extent that he mortgaged the farm for $3,000 to pay for the first printing of the Book of Mormon in 1830. Mrs. Harris left her husband as the result of his interest, he moved west and remarried, and the property changed owners. In 1849 the original wood Harris farmhouse burned, and Chapman had this house built of water-rounded vari-colored cobbles by mason Robert Johnson. The limestone quoins are painted white which is a twentieth century treatment favored by those owners wishing a stronger visual statement of the corners. In 1937 the property was acquired by the Church of the Latter Day Saints, which keeps it as a memorial to its forebears. It is open to the public. 39

8. WAYNE COUNTY, Keller House, 513 W. Maple Street, Newark

Construction of this house began in 1845 or 1846 for Jacob Keller who came to Newark from Columbia County. An old photograph (c. 1890) shows Eastlake style verandas spreading across the front and widely spaced wood brackets under the eaves. In the 1920s the house was acquired by an ancestor of the present owner. Architect I. Edgar Hill of Geneva was engaged at that time for renovations. He was responsible for the Greek Revival style entrance and porches which now grace the house. The cobblestones are the dark red water-rounded stones from Sodus which contrast effectively with the limestone quoins, lintels, sills, and water table.

9. WAYNE COUNTY, House, Old Route 31, Lyons Township

Built in 1834, this house has wood lintels spanning the windows. Roughly cut stone quoins, slightly smaller than those used in later buildings, form the corners.

10. WAYNE COUNTY, Green House, Dormedy Hill Road, Marion Township

The red water-rounded cobbles on this house, built in 1849 as noted on the stone tablet between the second floor windows at the right were undoubtedly brought down from Sodus Bay. The mason laid the stones on the left side in the herringbone pattern at the first floor level. The porch dates from the 1870s and may have replaced an earlier Greek Revival style porch.

11. WAYNE COUNTY, Hale Blacksmith Shop and House, Route 14, Alloway, Lyons Township

A date of 1827 has been given for these buildings, but it has not been proved nor disproved. The use of the octagonal shape is unusual for cobblestone buildings and especially a blacksmithy. One advantage of this shape is that cut stone quoins are not necessary to form the gentle corners. Across the road is the original blacksmith's house. Here the corners are stone quoins, roughly cut and varying slightly in size. The lintels in the house are wood planks, while those in the shop are wood timbers. Mortar joints in house and shop are not finished in the same manner, possibly indicating different construction dates and different masons.

44

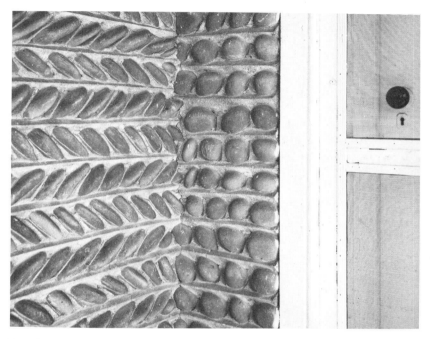

12, 13. WAYNE COUNTY, Baker House, Canandaigua Road, Macedon Township

This house, faced with small red water-rounded cobbles, was built in 1850 for J. Baker and is a slightly smaller version of the Hawks house in Ontario County. The wing at the left faced with oval stones laid in a herringbone pattern. Jacob Terry, the mason-builder, considered this house the best piece of work he had ever done. The front center porch is an early twentieth-century addition, a replacement for the original smaller porch.

LAKE ONTARIO PLAIN, WEST

Northwestern Monroe, Orleans, and Niagara Counties

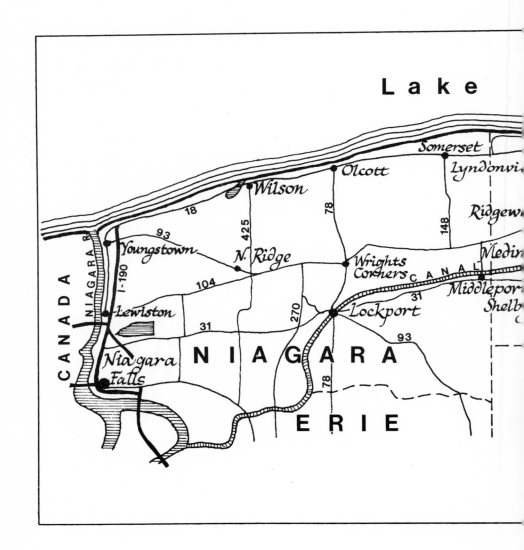

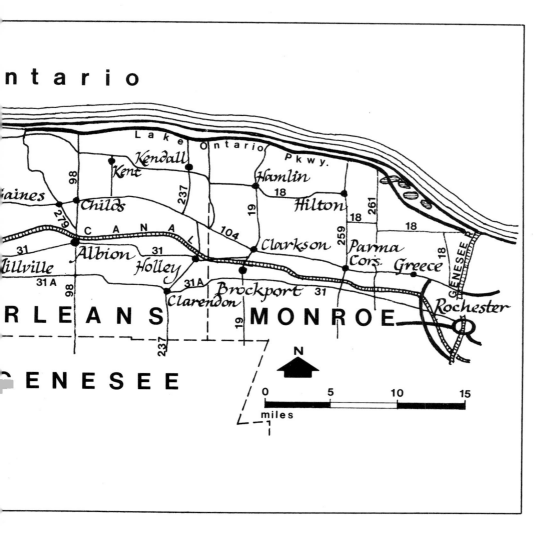

ntario

Lake Ontario Pkwy.

Kendall
Kent
Gaines
Childs
Hamlin
Hilton
86
237
18
19
261
279
C A N A L
104
Clarkson
259
Parma
Cors.
18
Genesee
Albion
31
31
Millville
Holley
Greece
18
31 A
98
31 A
Brockport
31
Clarendon
Rochester
RLEANS
237
19
M O N R O E

GENESEE

N

0   5   10   15

miles

14. Monroe County, Thrall House, 4929 Ridge Road (Route 104), Parma Township

Built in 1845, this is a Greek Revival version of the five-bay center-entrance house of the Georgian-Federal period. The porch is a handsome restoration of about 1950 that well fits the spirit of the house. Wooden panels below the first floor windows are unusual, and the frieze windows open into the attic. Cobbles are water-rounded stones. This cobblestone house is the first major cobblestone landmark encountered when driving west from Rochester along the historic Ridge Road.

51

15. Monroe County, House, Ridge Road (Route 104), Parma Township

The herringbone-patterned masonry was laid up in the late 1840s on the front wall of a house. The thin oval stones are sandstone, laid six courses per twelve-inch-high quoin.

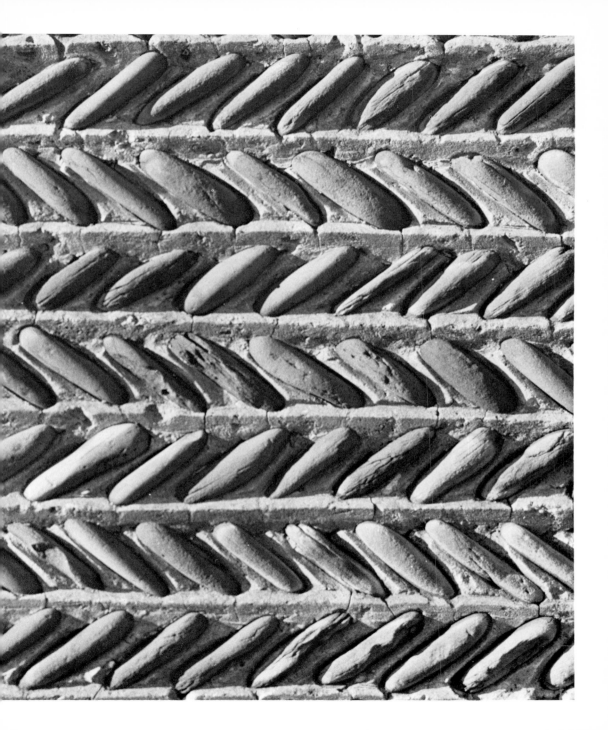

16. MONROE COUNTY, Crowell House, 9626 Ridge Road (Route 104), Clarkson Township

This house was probably built in the early 1830s. Its original owner was a doctor whose office was supposed to have been in the left wing. The walls of the wing are fieldstones, not cobbles, so this may have been built earlier than the main portion. The quoins are red sandstones, while the window and door lintels are brick. The cobbles themselves are of graduated size, smaller toward the top of the wall. There is no attempt to embellish the mortar joints. In the gable at the right-hand end of the house are small openings—two inches high and almost twelve inches long—supposedly to accommodate the bees whose hives were kept in the attic.

17. Monroe County, Johnson House, Detail, Orleans–Monroe County Line Road, Hamlin Township

Here water-rounded stones are laid with their long sides horizontal, except for the row immediately above the bottom quoin. The horizontal mortar joints are finished with a bead ½″ high. Quoins are red sandstone, 10″ high. This house was built in the mid 1840s.

18. ORLEANS COUNTY, **Blodget House, Ridge Road (Route 104), Murray
Township**

The stones of this 1840 house are rather smooth field cobbles accented with every
fourth row of horizontal water-rounded cobbles. The lintels are narrow water-
smoothed stones laid vertically to form a flat arch.

19. Orleans County, Proctor House, Childs, Ridge Road (Route 104), Gaines Township

Built in the mid-1840s of water-rounded cobbles, the form of this house—one floor with hipped roof over a high basement—is not often found in western New York. Brick lintels span the windows and door, a device found in several cobblestone buildings in this area. Horace Greeley held a mortgage on this house in the 1860s for a cousin who was then owner. In 1975 it was acquired by the Cobblestone Society, and the missing blinds and six-pane lower window sash have been restored. It is now a house-museum and office of the Society.

20. ORLEANS COUNTY, District 5 Schoolhouse, Ridge Road (Route 104), Childs, Gaines Township

Built in 1849, this building served as a school until 1952. It was acquired by the Cobblestone Society in 1961. The walls are only ten inches thick, including a six-inch veneer of water-rounded cobblestones fixed onto the wood construction. The tree in front was planted by one of the classes as part of its Arbor Day exercises, and it is one of the few that survived and grew. This schoolhouse retained its furnishings when it closed and now serves as a museum devoted to nineteenth-century education.

There were approximately fifty cobblestone school buildings constructed across upstate New York, most of them one-room schoolhouses. They gradually were closed as the result of the centralized school district program which started in the 1930s and many have been converted to residences.

59

21. ORLEANS COUNTY, First Univeralist Church, Ridge Road (Route 104), Childs, Gaines Township

Built in 1834, the church housed a congregation that could afford but few changes to the building as the century progressed. The stone and brick terrace and the stone steps to the door are the only changes to the exterior. In the early twentieth century the tower was removed rather than repaired. The impending sale and threatened destruction of this building in 1960 led to the formation of the Cobblestone Society which acquired it in 1963. The present tower, a gift of John D. Brush, was built in 1965, following an old photograph showing the original. The basement level contains the Cobblestone Society museum. This building is perhaps the best documented and best preserved example of an early cobblestone church.

23. ORLEANS COUNTY, Bullard House, Gaines Basin Road, Gaines Township

Cyrus Witheral was the mason of this house built in the early 1840s on which water-rounded cobbles face the front wall. Side and rear walls are of uncoursed cobbles much larger than those on the front. The glass in the sidelights of the entrance are 7″ x 9″ panes set one directly upon another with no wood muntins.

2. ORLEANS COUNTY, Hall House, Detail, Ridge Road (Route 104), Gaines Township

Here, in a house built in the early 1840s, are two cobblestone patterns. The foundation, below the stone water table utilizes large water-rounded stones with all mortar joints given equal emphasis, resulting in a honeycomb pattern. The main wall above the water table is composed of oval water-rounded stones set vertically. The horizontal mortar joints are finished with a bead. This use of oval stones set vertically is found in several buildings in Orleans and Niagara counties.

24. ORLEANS COUNTY, Bacon House, Brown Road, Gaines Township

This house was built in two stages, the right wing being built first about 1840. Construction of the main part began in 1851 for Hosea Bacon, who kept an account book which survives in the possession of descendants. James Thompson was the mason, and he started work in mid-April, finishing on September 15, 1851. In addition to $55.92 "hard money," Thompson received butter, corn, cornmeal, and wheat. Orrin Beach, a carpenter, worked from September 18 to December 17, 1851, before stopping for the winter. He resumed work on April 12 and finished on July 21, 1852. Beach received $141.56 "hard money," beef, apples, lard, pigs, salertus, wheat, and pork. This was probably the usual length of time for construction of a cobblestone building. The water-rounded stones, for which Bacon provided the transportation, were gathered on the shore of Lake Ontario, near Kent, seven miles north. It is not recorded, but it is possible that the cast iron grilles at the frieze windows came from Bacon's foundry about a mile away. The porch fronting the wing is a twentieth-century addition.

25. ORLEANS COUNTY, Whipple House, Detail, Ridge Road (Route 104), Gaines Township

Here, water-smoothed stones, ½″–1″ thick have been laid in a herringbone pattern. The sandstone quoins are twelve inches high. This house is similar in overall form to the Parker house (Plate 27), but the Whipple house has a larger cornice and a wider, recessed entrance. It was built in the mid 1840s.

26. ORLEANS COUNTY, Saunders House, Ridge Road (Route 104), Gaines Township

This is one of the rare three-part houses: a two-and-one-half-story central part and a one-and-one-half-story wing at each side. The house was built in 1844 for Isaac Saunders. Cyrus Witheral was one of the masons, and it is assumed he was responsible for the herringbone pattern of the central section (see Plates 25 and 27). He was paid $75 for his work. The two side wings are faced with oval water-rounded stones. We see in this building the heavy wood cornice and an entrance of the Greek Revival style. The fan-shaped ornament in the gable end is a carry-over from the earlier Federal style.

27. ORLEANS COUNTY, Parker House, Swett Road, Ridgeway Township

This house, built c. 1845, utilizes the herringbone pattern on the front wall and up in the gable end on the side wall. The sandstone quoins are unusually large—eighteen inches high and twenty-two inches long. Most stone quoins are twelve inches high and eighteen inches long. The wooden rear wing has a cobblestone foundation. There are a number of wood Greek Revival farmhouses in western New York with the exposed masonry foundations faced with cobblestones.

28. ORLEANS COUNTY, Millville Academy, Millville, Route 31A, Shelby Township

The airiness of the open cupola, housing a school bell, contrasts delightfully with the solidity of the field cobble walls. Built in 1840, this building originally housed an academy. Academies were established by public subscription in many New York State communities in the early nineteenth century and offered their students a secondary education. The Millville Academy offered a curriculum of mathematics and moral sciences. In 1849 it had an enrollment of 59 females and 113 males. Tuition ranged from $1.72–$6.19 per course per semester. Boarding students were accommodated in nearby homes. The advent of the state's normal school system sounded the death knell for academies, and the Millville Academy eventually became a district school. The building is now owned by the Millville United Methodist Church and used for church dinners as well as for community functions. The present cupola dates from district school days, the compass points are gone but the arrow still turns into the wind.

69

29. ORLEANS COUNTY, Grinnell House, Millville, East Shelby Road, Shelby Township

The unique feature of this façade of water-rounded stones is the ornamentation worked in the stones. The mason took small oval stones and set them vertically in rows between the lintels. In addition to the herringbone pattern in the gable end, there is a half-circle of three rows of stones over the door. The center row is round stones, flanked by rows of vertical oval stones. The house was built about 1845.

30. ORLEANS COUNTY, Blood House, 142 South Main Street, Lyndonville

The massiveness of the cornice on this house is indicative of the end of the Greek Revival era, although its size is somewhat minimized by dark paint. The house was built about 1850 of very small, carefully sized water-rounded stones. The stone band that springs across the second floor windows is unique.

31. ORLEANS COUNTY, Blood House, Detail

This is a detail of the masonry of the rear wall. The various sizes and shapes of the cobbles are a marked contrast to those in the front wall. The coarseness of the mortar is typical of that used in cobblestone walls. The honeycomb pattern was not generally used on front walls in Orleans County, except for foundations. The speckled or mottled cobbles are much harder Canadian metamorphic rocks than the darker, solid color cobbles, which are local red sandstone, a softer sedimentary rock. All, however, are smooth water-rounded cobblestones.

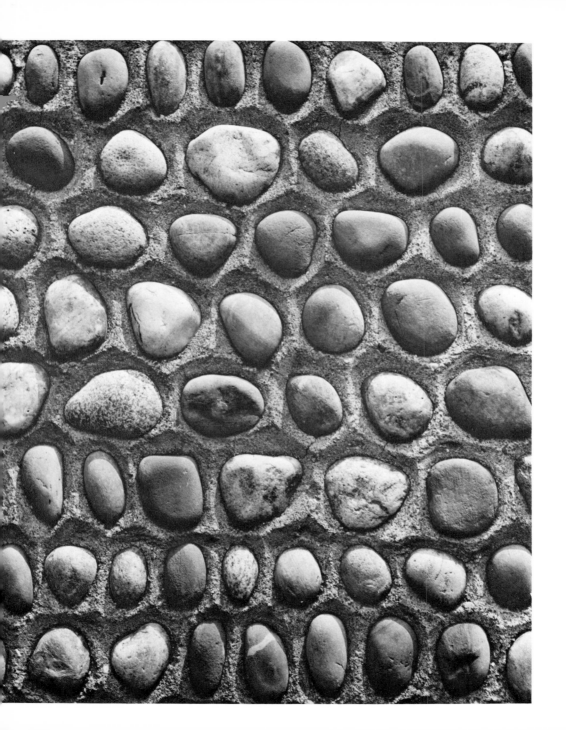

32. Niagara County, First Universalist Church, South Main Street, Middleport, Royalton Township

The water-rounded cobbles for this 1841 building were collected from the Lake Ontario shore at congregational picnics organized for this purpose. The gray oval stones in the panels between the stone pilasters are set vertically (see Plate 22). Fred Shy was the mason. The capitals of the two free-standing Doric columns are circular, as are those of the columns marking the corners of the hexagonal cupola. The design for this building came from Asher Benjamin's *The Builders' Guide,* first published in 1839.

33. NIAGARA COUNTY, Babcock House, 7749 Lake Road (Route 19), Somerset Township

The water-rounded cobbles of this house are laid horizontally. Doric columns support an entablature which is slightly set back over the door, a favorite treatment seen on many Greek Revival houses in Niagara County. Behind the storm door is the original front door which has two narrow panels, typical of the Greek Revival style. Wood grilles front the frieze windows which light the second floor bedrooms of this 1840 building.

34. NIAGARA COUNTY, Whatlock House, 2449 Maple Road, Wilson Township
The outstanding features of this house are the Doric columned porch at the front entrance and the sawed wood grilles at the frieze windows. The cobbles are water-rounded stones. The blinds are twentieth-century replacements of the louvered nineteenth-century originals. Foundation stones are small, naturally rectangular stones which are coursed. There are several houses in this area which are entirely faced with these stones and the mortar joints given the same treatment as in a cobblestone building.

35. Niagara County, Johnson House, Route 425, Wilson Township

This house is a monumental cottage. The great frieze of the Greek Revival cornices masks a full-height second floor. Here the grilles of the frieze windows are cast iron. The cut limestone of the entrance and window lintels is extremely fine workmanship. The water-rounded cobbles of the front wall are extremely small, laid six courses to each quoin. Morgan Johnson, a ship captain, had this house built in 1844.

GENESEE REGION

Southern Monroe, Genesee, Livingston, and Wyoming Counties

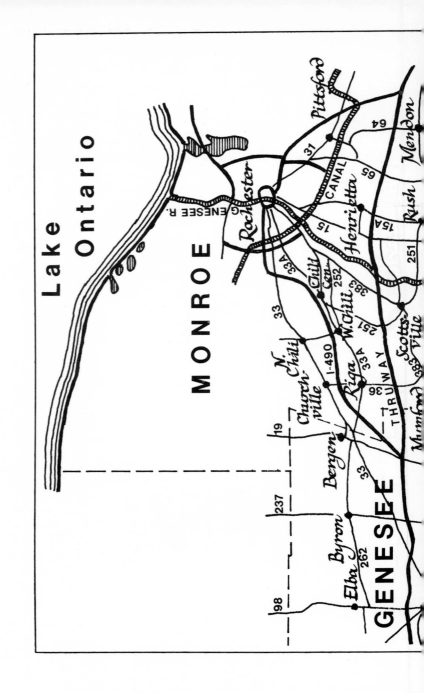

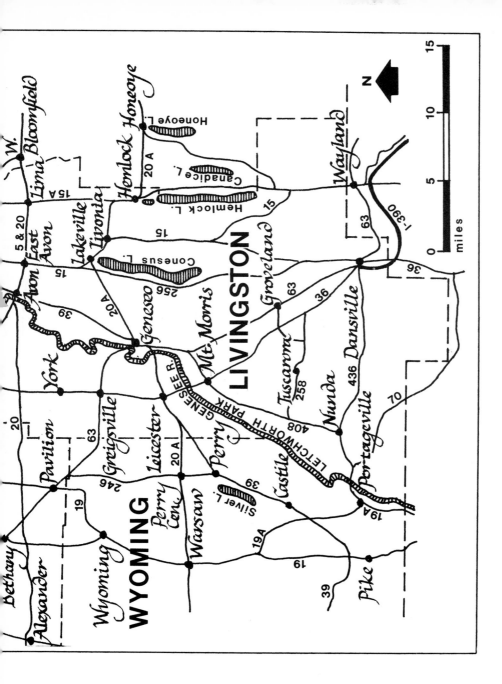

81

36, 37. MONROE COUNTY, Quaker Meeting House, 459 Quaker Road, Wheatland Township

Built of field cobbles in 1834 as a meeting house for a group of Orthodox Quakers, this building was used by the group for twenty years. Then it became the meeting house for a group of liberal, Hicksite Quakers for twenty years. Subsequently, it became the meeting place of the local Grange and is now a residence. The Quaker origin shows in the two entrances—one for women, the other for men—and the simplicity of the building.

38. MONROE COUNTY, Cox House, 5015 River Road, Wheatland Township

Isaac Cox, a pioneer Quaker settler, arrived in the area in 1804. His success as a what farmer and profits from the Scottsville flour mill enabled him to build this field cobble house in 1839. It was built as a double house, Isaac living in one half and one of his sons in the other half. The handsome porches with their square columns are original. At each upper corner of the stone lintel over the front door are the wrought-iron X-shaped ends of tie rods which were run through the building sometime in the last century to arrest a bulging rear wall.

39. Monroe County, Sheffer House, 95 Sheffer Road, Chili Township

The mood of this house is relaxed by the off-center entrance and window above it, resulting from floor plan requirements. It was built of field cobbles between 1835 and 1840. The blinds with adjustable louvers are original and are the type used on many buildings constructed before the Civil War.

40. Monroe County, Tinker House, 1585 Calkins Road, Henrietta Township

James Tinker came from New Haven, Connecticut, in 1812 and in 1830 had this house built by a mason named McCarty. The stones are rather large field cobbles, although the eight-inch quoins are not as high as those in later houses. The arch of the simple Federal entrance is formed of roughly cut tapered stones. Window lintels, likewise, are the flat arch type, made of roughly cut tapered stones. In later houses the stone was more finely cut. The front door retains its original pair of louvered blinds with curved tops to fit the opening. Their original function was to provide ventilation during the summer.

41. Monroe County, **Bullard House, 830 Telephone Road, Henrietta Township**

This Federal entrance with its half-elliptical fanlight is perhaps the most elaborate of a group of these entrances built in this area. The fanlight has leaded glass—most of the others have wood muntins—while the sidelights have simple rectangular glass panes separated by wood muntins. Reeded pilasters flank door and sidelights. The house was built in the 1830s.

42. Monroe County, Bettridge House, 253 Bettridge Road, Riga Township

William Emmons, a mason, was the nephew of the two Bettridge brothers who settled on this road and gave their name to it. They came from England and eventually sent for their nephew, who built this house for William Bettridge sometime in the 1830s. The front door, for once not obscured by a storm or screen door, shows itself to be one of the favored designs of the Greek Revival period—two narrow vertical panels. The entrance is typically Federal in style, with both fanlight and sidelights admitting ample light into the central entrance hall, although it is unusual in having cut stone completely frame the opening. The blinds on the first floor windows, apparently original, are atypical in each having three louvered sections instead of the usual two, as seen on the second floor windows.

43. Monroe County, Church House, 6710 Chili-Riga Road (Route 33A), Riga Township

Elihu Church, for whom Churchville was named, arrived from Ware, Massachusetts, in 1806. Sometime between 1832 and 1836 he had this house built. Although an unsigned drawing of the front elevation and floor plan exist in the house, its designer is unknown. The main portion of the house is square. On the rear is an L-shaped wing, also of field cobbles, which originally housed a summer kitchen, milk room, and woodshed. Symmetry is maintained on the front with a false window to the left of the recessed porch. The two columns are of stone. The form of the house is unique among cobblestone buildings. The dormers are later additions to provide light to the second floor which was converted from an attic to additional bedrooms.

44. MONROE COUNTY, Hartwell House, Hartwell Road, Rush Township

Built in the mid-1830s of field cobbles, this is a simple, serene house of great dignity with decorative emphasis centered on the front door. This cut-stone framed opening has a pair of narrow doors under the semicircular top. The use of stone quoins at each side of the door is unusual.

45. Genesee County, "Castleton" Ford House, 4899 Ford Road (Route 262), Elba Township

In 1841 Nathaniel Ford had this house built, naming it "Castleton," almost twenty years after he had come to the area. The field cobbles have a natural rectangularity (almost square corners) which are also found in certain parts of Wyoming and Livingston counties. The Greek Revival entrance is particularly handsome. The old cobblestone walk was uncovered during the recent restoration, showing a rare use of such stone for other than buildings in upstate New York.

46. Genesee County, Alexander Classical School, Alexander

This is probably the largest cobblestone school building constructed. It was originally a private school like the Millville Academy (Plate 28). Built in 1837, it had an enrollment of 300 students in the 1850s, including some from southern states, but became a public school after the Civil War. The balustrade and the domed octagonal cupola—originally housing the school bell—appropriately crown the building. The building now serves as Alexander Town Hall, with a museum of local history occupying the top floor.

47. Livingston County, Hayden House, River Road, York Township

Moses Hayden, first judge of the county, had this house built of field cobbles about 1840. It is easy to speculate that the building's location in the Genesee Valley and the social position of its first owner are responsible for its pretentiousness. The Genesee Valley produced a number of buildings with a special stamp of quality during the nineteenth century. All of the window and door openings of the Hayden house are framed with cut stone, including the basement windows. The pediment of the portico is faced with cobblestones and has an oval window as its central ornament. The twinned chimney stacks and the ample overhang of the roof are later modifications. This building is now part of the Trappist Abbey of the Genesee.

48. LIVINGSTON COUNTY, Ramsdell Store, Route 36, York Village

This simple, handsome building was constructed of field cobbles c. 1840 to serve as a village store, which accounts for the slightly wider-than-usual windows and numerous doors. A cut-stone watertable girdles the building at the first floor line, and the doorways still retain their paneled reveals. It has also served as a post office and a barbershop.

49. LIVINGSTON COUNTY, Geneseo District No. 5 Schoolhouse, Center Street, Geneseo

Construction of this schoolhouse was started in 1838 and presumably was completed by winter of the same year. The form of the building is unique, with its two wings and hipped roofs. Now, as headquarters of the Livingston County Historical Society, it is a museum open to the public.

50. LIVINGSTON COUNTY, Wadsworth House, West Lake Road, Geneseo Township

This house has a certain kinship with Design XVIII in *The Architecture of Country Houses,* first published in 1850, of the great American tastemaker of the 1840s and 50s, A. J. Downing. Downing called this design "a bracketed farm-house in the American Style—"American" because he showed his house constructed of wood, exhibiting "no ostentation unbecoming an American farmer." This house, built of field cobbles, commands handsome prospects to the east and south of Conesus Lake. It was probably built in the early 1850s.

51. WYOMING COUNTY, Taber House, Middle Reservation Road (County Road 6), Castile Township

The form of this Greek Revival house is rare in cobblestone buildings: two-story central section with recessed porch, one story wings on each side, and hipped roofs on all three parts. The gray and tan field cobbles have a natural rectangularity, similar to those in Castleton (Plate 45). The date stone of 1844 is between the two second-floor windows.

52. Wyoming County, Cox House, East Bethany Road, Middlebury Township

Only the front wall of this 1835 house is of cobbles—3,000 large ones, with but two courses per quoin. The side wall is a rubble stone wall of small boulders, many having been split to make a flat exterior wall surface. This side wall is what the stone wall behind the cobblestone facing looks like.

FINGER LAKES

Steuben, Ontario, Seneca, Cayuga, and Yates Counties

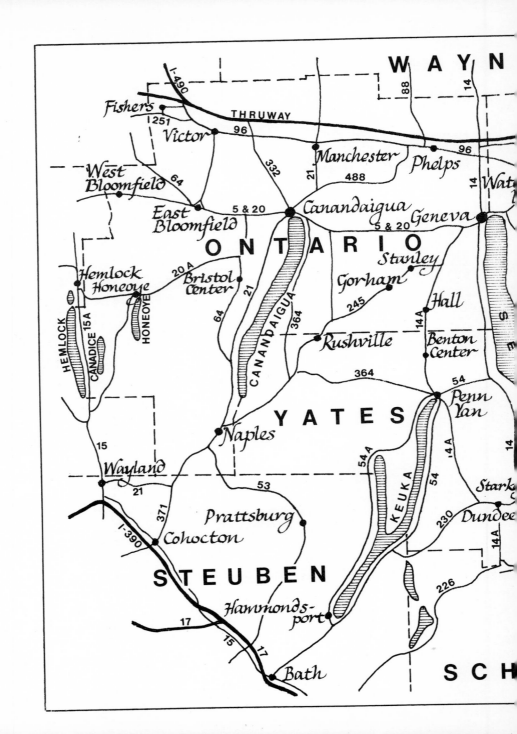

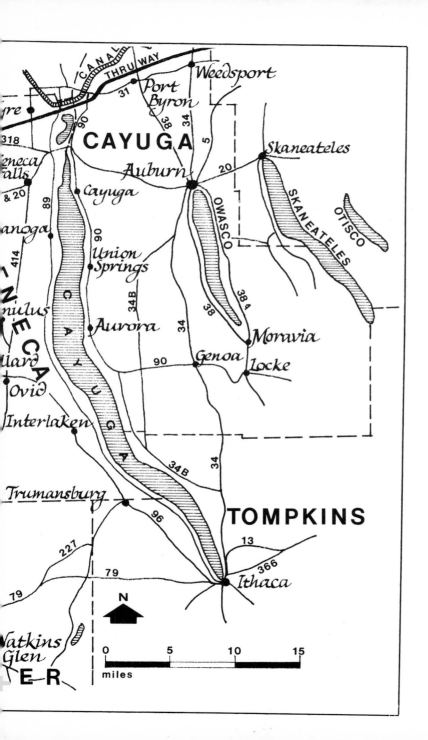

53. STEUBEN COUNTY, Barnes House, 120 West Washington Boulevard, Bath

Bath, as county seat and center of development in the early nineteenth century of this part of New York State, is a town where people lived with a special sense of social customs and a bit of aplomb. In 1851 County Judge Washington Barnes had this house built for him by Willington Salt. One glance tells that Barnes was a man of some stature in the community. The scale of the building is quite ample, with first floor ceilings more than twelve feet high. The dentils at the main cornice are a nice refinement—and added expense. The porch is an early twentieth-century addition.

54, 55. Ontario County, Herendeen House, County Road 8, Canandaigua Township

This is one of the earliest cobblestone houses built in Ontario County, as indicated by the 1832 datestone over the door. Field cobbles were used to face the house, and the quoins are roughly squared limestone of varying size. Occurring at intervals on the front of the building are "pugging holes" which supported the scaffolding used to construct the walls. These holes were virtually always filled in upon completion of the masonry when the scaffolding was dismantled. The stone piers at the corners of the front terrace date from the early twentieth century.

The photograph of the side door gives an idea of the thickness of the walls. It also shows the rough texture and the larger cobbles used on side and rear walls.

56. ONTARIO COUNTY, Jenks Store, 6451 Victor-Manchester Road (Route 96), Victor Township

Businesses have been housed in this handsome building since the mid-1830s. The details of the cornice are in the Federal style and contrast with the massiveness of the cut stone piers and stone entablature below. Notice that the first floor windows and door are recessed with paneled wood reveals, while the second floor windows are almost flush with the face of the field cobblestones. While the concrete platform and steps that front the building are of comparatively recent origin, they had counterparts originally in wood. Except for the advertising, the building presents much the same aspect in the twentieth century that it did in the nineteenth century.

57, 58. ONTARIO COUNTY, Insurance Office, Route 5 and Route 20, West Bloomfield

At first glance one would probably surmise that this was originally the village school house. But the elliptical stone panel over the door states that it was "Ont. & Liv. Mutual Insurance Office A D 1841" (Ontario & Livingston). The roof has lost its Greek Revival cornice, probably shortly after the Civil War when the eaves were extended to give a more fashionable overhang.

The front wall of the building is faced with the smallest stones used in a cobblestone structure: 8–11 courses to the quoin (which is twelve inches high). The quoins are limestone, somewhat roughly squared.

59. Ontario County, House, West Swamp Road, Gorham Township

With little pretension, sitting placidly on a gentle rise, this house of field cobbles has changed hardly at all since its construction in the 1840s. It is fortunate in retaining its original porch. Shutters on the frieze windows, above the porch roof, are unusual. For symmetry's sake a false window (with the closed shutters) is on the left-hand end wall.

60. Ontario County, Bonsteel House, High Street and Turk Hill Road, Victor

In 1842 P. S. Bonsteel described the building of his house in a letter to *The Cultivator*, a magazine devoted to farming and related matters. He had built the house in 1835 and was very proud of it. He went on to say: "The stone I do not consider any expense as it frees the land of them. There is no painting to be done to it, as is required of brick or wood, it makes the strongest of walls, and I think the neatest and cheapest building that can be made." By 1878, when it was illustrated in the Ontario County Atlas, the house had had its eaves extended, a wooden second floor added to the rear wing, and an Italianate front porch added. These changes survive to this day.

61. ONTARIO COUNTY, First Baptist Church, Church Street, Phelps

The Greek Revival style provides a dignified form for a house of worship. This one was built in 1845. Originally it was called "Baptist Chapel," but it later became a "church," perhaps when the window sash and clear glass were changed to stained glass sometime after the Civil War. The front wall and one side wall are red water-rounded stones, while the other side wall is faced with multicolored stones. Note the scalloped edge of the louvers in the cupola, making a fish scale pattern. The handsome ornament in the pediment, comprised of scrolls and an anthemion, has no particular religious significance. Stone quoins at each side of the doorway provide an additional bit of emphasis at this point.

62. ONTARIO COUNTY, Hoffman House, Ontario-Seneca County Line Road, Phelps Township

Water-rounded cobbles from Lake Ontario's shore face the walls of this house built in 1845. Slightly darker brown cobbles face the upper part of the front wall, which may indicate a different beach on Lake Ontario as their origin. The broad triangular window, lighting the attic, is found in several Greek Revival houses in this area. The house is a typical New York State farm house in plan—L-shaped, with a two-and-one-half-story main portion and a one-and-one-half-story wing.

63. ONTARIO COUNTY, Hoffman House Entrance

This entrance is remarkable for it is all of cut stone, including the entrance steps
and platform. The original owner, William Hoffman, had his initials and construction date, 1845, carved into the frieze over the door. The delicate curved lines in
the sidelights are thin wood strips applied on the outside of the glass.

64. Ontario County, Smith House, Maryland Street, Phelps Township

A datestone set into the wall above the door proclaims that this house was built in 1841. It is distinguished by oval field cobbles laid in a herringbone pattern on the front wall. Up in the gable end on the side wall is a circular ornament worked in cobblestones.

65. Ontario County, House, Pinewood Cemetery Road, Phelps Township

The simple Federal entrance would indicate that this house was built in the early 1830s. The field cobbles are almost rectangular and give a smooth texture to the walls. The lintels are roughly cut limestones forming a flat arch. The large overhang of the roof is a post–Civil War extension found on many early nineteenth-century buildings across New York State. Country roads in the northern Ontario County townships of Phelps, Farmington, and Manchester offer a wide range of cobblestone buildings.

66. ONTARIO COUNTY, Hawks House, Route 96, Phelps Township

Here the basic cottage form, one and one-half stories, has gone Gothic. By placing a gable in the center and interrupting the eave at each side with a dormer, the roof is given the picturesque quality championed by A. J. Downing in the 1840s and 50s. Downing disliked Greek Revival and wrote widely read books and articles espousing new styles, particularly Gothic Revival. Hawks built his cottage in 1848 of dark red water-rounded cobbles from the Sodus area.

67. Ontario County, Hawks House Window

The curved head of the original Gothic window style is here simplified to straight lines. The pointed top is emphasized by three rows of cobbles which follow the profile of the top. The louvered blinds are original.

68. Ontario County, Hawks House, Detail,

69. ONTARIO COUNTY, King House, Route 96, Phelps Township

The plowed field, strewn with cobblestone glacial residue, graphically shows the abundance of the building material. This house and connected cobblestone barns form an ensemble unique in New York State. They were built in the early 1840s. Since this photograph was taken in the 1950s, concrete buttresses have been added to bolster the walls of the barns.

70. Ontario County, Tiffany House, 1900 Macedon Road, Canandaigua Township

It is the central projection that gives this house (c. 1845) distinction. At the first floor of this projection, under a handsome porch with a curious mansard roof, a pair of doors serve as main entrance. Above this, at the second floor level, the central window has an inswinging sash—the influence of French architectural styles.

71. Ontario County, Tiffany House, Corner Detail

Most cobblestone buildings have smaller stones on the front wall and larger ones on the side walls as shown in this photograph. The quoins are twelve inches high, and they have tooled borders and panels frequently used on cut stone trim for buildings constructed during the first half of the nineteenth century. The irregularities in the field cobbles clearly show.

72. Ontario County, House Entrance, Fox Road, Farmington Township
Cut stone pilasters and entablature emphasize this entrance. This rendition in stone is paralleled by similar and more numerous versions in wood on many Greek Revival buildings in central and western New York.

73. ONTARIO COUNTY, Barron House, Route 5 and Route 20, Seneca Township

The Barron family arrived in this area from England in the late 1790s, settled here, and built a log cabin on the site. They prospered at farming and built this house, incising "T. Barron 1848" in the lintel over the main door, the date being the year construction was started. Construction of the house took two years, and family records noted the cost as $2,100. The red water-rounded cobbles came from Sodus on Lake Ontario, making the trip in wagons that hauled Barron wheat to this port. This form of house—two-story central section with portico and one-and-one-half-story wings—was a favored form for the more imposing houses of the Greek Revival era. The door in the left wing is a false door to balance that in the right wing. The brick steps and porch floors are twentieth century replacements of the wood originals.

74. ONTARIO COUNTY, Tucker-Lewis House, Pre-Emption Road, Geneva Township

Silas Tucker purchased the farm from his father-in-law Jephthah Earl in 1826. Both men later built impressive cobblestone houses, Tucker building first, in 1838. The Tucker farmhouse is illustrated in an 1876 atlas—*Ontario County History*. It was distinguished by a double porch on the south end (at the left, behind the tree). In 1905 Katherine Belle Lewis, then owner, doubled the size of the house with an extension to the north (right) and a porch on the east side which is the central feature in the photograph. This porch is a duplicate of the 1838 porch. The original end of Tucker's house is behind the second column from the right. Katherine Lewis had her enlargement constructed by the same methods and materials as those originally used—field cobbles, lime mortar, and limestone lintels and quoins. In addition to enlarging the house, she had two other cobblestone buildings constructed on the property. One was a gatehouse, destroyed by fire some years ago; the other is a two-story gardenhouse. The buildings are well hidden from the road, settled back into a 600-acre estate.

75, 76. ONTARIO COUNTY, Tucker-Lewis House

Cut limestone quoins make the corners on the house, both the original portion and the 1905 enlargement. On a two-story garden house which Mrs. Lewis had built in 1906 or '07 the cobblestones themselves form the corners. This treatment is unique in New York State, but several examples occur on Wisconsin's cobblestone buildings.

126

77. ONTARIO COUNTY, Barnes House, Pre-Emption Road, Geneva Township

Barnes started the construction of his house in 1835 and completed it in 1838. He was partial to the Ionic column, and it is used on the two-story portico, the main entrance, and the porch of the wing, as well as on mantels of two fireplaces inside. Compare the pediment of this portico with that on the Barron house (Plate 73) to see the change of Greek Revival design in a ten-year period.

78. ONTARIO COUNTY, Rippey House, Route 245 and Leet Road, Seneca Township

J. Rippey, Jr., was evidently very proud when he had his house built for he had his name and date (1854) incised in the lintel over the front door. For this house the fifteenth- and sixteenth-century Italian villas of the Tuscan hills served as inspiration. Massive sawed brackets of wood support the overhang of the eaves (the brackets of the Tuscan villas never were as exuberant as these American descendants). The windows in the main portion find their ancestors in the early renaissance Florentine palazzi. The masonry is extremely fine, the red water-rounded cobbles evidently came from Sodus in Lake Ontario. They are carefully matched for uniformity and laid with utmost regularity. The limestone trim is also uniform in color and carefully cut. In the front gable end the round attic window has been transformed into an unblinking eye, with a mortar "white," that stares over the road and fields beyond.

79. ONTARIO COUNTY, Rippey House Window

Windows of Italian buildings of the fifteenth and sixteenth centuries were the models for this window. A pair of round arched sash are contained beneath one over-spanning arch formed with a double row of narrow oval cobblestones. This pattern of arches is repeated by the muntins at the top of the upper sash.

80. **ONTARIO COUNTY, Pumphouse for Railroad, Route 96, Fishers, Town of Victor**

The Erie Canal was one of the prime factors in bringing about cobblestone masonry, and the railroad gradually brought about the eclipse of the canal as the main artery across upstate New York. A minor paradox, therefore, is this small structure erected in 1850 to slake the thirst of railroad engines. Now the railroad tracks are gone, leaving the building "beached" high and dry.

A historical marker placed here by the State Education Department in 1932 reads:

Ground for Auburn-Rochester Railroad
broken here. First train Sept. 10, 1840
Chester Fisher, first agent

81. SENECA COUNTY, Lay House, Lay Road and Mays Point Road, Tyre Township

Hiram Lay had this house built of field cobbles about 1847. The cupola crowning the house was originally on one of his wood barns, now demolished. A cobblestone carriage house also built by him still stands nearby and is now part of the Montezuma National Wildlife Refuge. A drawing showing the entire farm building complex appears in the 1876 *Seneca County History*.

82. Seneca County, First Methodist Episcopal Church, Old State Road, Junius Township

Built of field cobbles in 1839 as noted on the stone tablet between the doors, this church is unusual in having two doors. The original pulpit may have been inside, between these two doors and under the oval window now glazed with stained glass. Originally a wooden porch with wooden steps on all three sides stretched across the entire front.

83. Cayuga County, Allen House, Route 90, Ledyard Township

This house was built c. 1850 of red, water-rounded cobbles, undoubtedly from Sodus on Lake Ontario. The trinity of gables stretch their necks above an Eastlake style (c. 1890) porch to see Cayuga Lake across the road. The windows all have triangular louvered panels above them in the effort to simulate the lancet windows of the Gothic period.

84. CAYUGA COUNTY, Reynolds House, Center Road, Scipio Township

A Mr. Reynolds reportedly had this house built for his son-in-law and daughter
c. 1845. Reynolds was evidently pleased with his son-in-law or perhaps more
concerned about the home for his daughter, for this is a large, impressive house.
The substantial cornice is a hallmark of the Green Revival style. Surrounding the
recessed entrance is a simple cut stone border which contrasts effectively with the
field cobbles.

85. YATES COUNTY, Earl House, Route 14, Benton Township

Jephthah Earl, father-in-law of Silas Tucker, had his house built of red water-rounded cobbles from Sodus Bay about 1850. It sits on a gentle rise of ground looking across the road to Seneca Lake. The details on this house are a remarkable collection of styles. The cornices start out being Greek Revival, but the eaves project further than the Greek Revival norm. These eaves are given visual support by closely spaced wood brackets—brackets of a different profile and closer spacing than seen in an Italianate building. The porch columns have fluted shafts with capitals which might be called Egyptian Revival.

86. YATES COUNTY, Spence House, Lakemont-Himrod Road, Starkey Township

A mason named Lemoreaux built this house in 1848 of water-rounded red sand-stone cobbles from the Sodus area on Lake Ontario. It remained in the family of the original owner—Dr. Henry Spence—for a century and a quarter. The great cornice marks the final flowering of the Greek Revival style and gives an almost overpowering monumentality to the house. There are two wings at the rear of the main block of the house, making it U-shape in plan.

87. YATES COUNTY, Spence House

Here, in a side view of the house, one of the two rear wings is shown. The great brick-bordered oval opening in the main portion has lost its original sash. Water running off the rear wing roof and down the main wall has caused a portion of the cobblestone facing to fall away, exposing the face of the rubble stone behind.

EASTERN REVERBERATIONS

Onondaga, Madison, Oneida, Montgomery, and Albany Counties

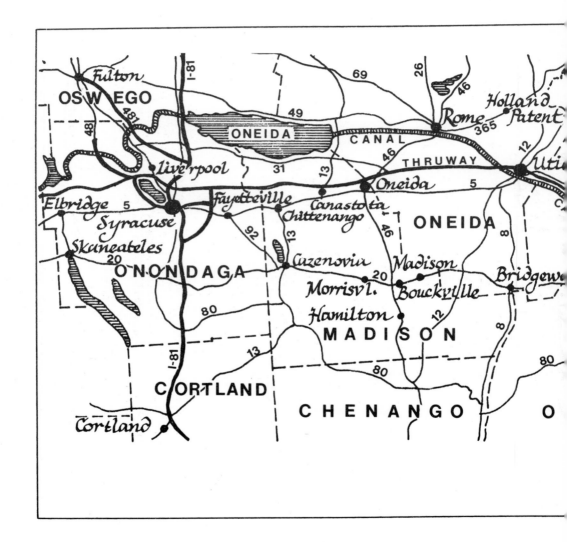

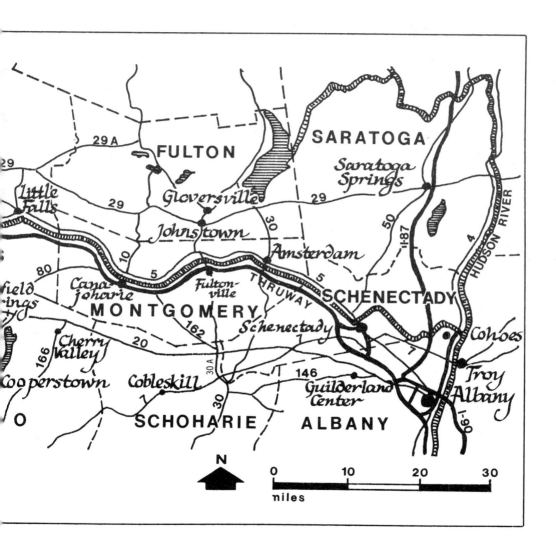

N

0   10   20   30

niles

145

88. Onondaga County, Munro House, Route 5, Elbridge

The Munro family was important in the development of this area, settling here in 1799. By the mid-nineteenth century they had prospered to such extent that John Munro, one of four sons of the original Munro, felt a new home properly befitting a man of his position was in order. He had Thomas Atkinson, an architect who came from England, design the residence and stay with him during the two years it took to build this house, 1850–51. The water-rounded cobblestones are very small and came from Lake Ontario near Oswego. Their color is mostly greenish gray. The roofing is slate and apparently original. Diamond-paned sash, filling all the window openings, are also original.

89. ONONDAGA COUNTY, Munro House

This is scholarly Gothic. Architect Thomas Atkinson brought with him English architectural books and a first-hand knowledge of English Gothic buildings. The vergeboards, the oriel window, the Tudor (ogival) arch, the diamond-paned sash, and stacked chimneys all combine to form an extremely effective composition.

147

90. ONONDAGA COUNTY, Munro House, Detail

The different textures of water-rounded cobbles, old mortar, and stone quoins clearly show in this photograph. The new mortar patching in the vertical crack at the left shows the smoother texture of modern Portland cement.

91. Onondaga County, Campbell Family Mausoleum, Old Elbridge Cemetery, Route 5, Elbridge Township

The curved top of the front wall, built in 1879, is echoed in the curved lower wing walls which are built of rectangular stones. The field cobble facing gives extra emphasis to the central portion. Time and weather have not dealt too kindly with the horizontal mortar joints on this portion, causing parts of them to erode.

92. ONONDAGA COUNTY, Hicks House, 600 Vine Street, Liverpool

One does not often find unequal spacing of the columns of a two-story portico. It was done here to give proper framing to the main entrance. The columned side porch turns the corner and marches to the rear of the building. Jonathan Hicks is supposed to have been the first owner of this house, built about 1854 of water-rounded cobbles. He was the owner of the National Hotel, also built of cobble-stones, although the hotel has not been as splendidly cared for as the house.

93. ONONDAGA COUNTY, National Hotel, 400 First Street, Liverpool

This is Jonathan Hicks's National Hotel as it originally appeared and pictured on this old post card, courtesy of the Onondaga Historical Association. It was built of field cobbles in 1839 from a design by H. and W. Clark, architects. The building still stands but bears changes made by various owners.

94. Madison County, Beckwith House, Route 92, Cazenovia Township

This typical upstate New York farmhouse has a certain elegance for which the Cazenovia area is noted. The proportions are ample, the main entrance has sidelights, Doric columns, and transom, and the porch of the side wing also has Doric columns. This Greek Revival house of water-rounded cobbles was built about 1840.

95. MADISON COUNTY, Coolidge Building, Route 20 and Canal Road, Bouckville

Built in 1847, this structure originally served as stores and residences. The manner in which the building turns the corner is unique. The cupola, with its diamond-shaped windows looks like a great masked head staring out over road and village. The limestone quoins, alternately long and short, are unusual. The owner, James E. Coolidge (who introduced hop growing to New York State), chose his site carefully for a commerical block—it stands at the crossing of the north-south Chenango Valley Canal and U.S. Route 20, the Cherry Valley Turnpike.

96. Madison County, House, Route 20, Madison

The vogue for building octagonal houses swept across the state, and country, about the same time as the vogue for building cobblestone houses. Orson Squire Fowler popularized the octagonal house through writings and lectures. The corners of this house are formed with limestone quoins. The entrance is Greek Revival, with two complete diminutive Doric columns at each side of the door. Molding profiles are Greek Revival. If the roof projection, with its brackets, is original it foretells the coming of the Italianate style. The house is supposed to have been built in 1840, and it is also reputed to have an air space in the exterior walls for added insulation.

97. ONEIDA COUNTY, Hop Dryer, Route 8, north of Bridgewater

Hops were an important cash crop before the Civil War in central and western New York. Structures for their drying, usually built of wood, were found throughout the region. This one is unique for its circular form and for its cobblestone exterior. The two metal bands girdling the structure were added at a later date, presumably to contain a bulge. There are records in the Cobblestone Society's files of circular schoolhouses in two counties which have been demolished.

98. ONEIDA COUNTY, House, Main Street (Route 365), Holland Patent

Great cobblestone cylindrical shafts rising up to cut stone Doric capitals support a pediment whose tympanum is also cobblestone. These stone shafts effectively set off the handsome Greek Revival entrance which has carved ornamentation (barely discernable) in the main entablature and the pilasters flanking the door. Although the name of the original owner of the house is unknown, the name of the mason is not—he was William J. Babcock. Babcock was born in Petersburg, Rensselaer County, New York. At the age of twenty-one he built two stone factory buildings at North Adams and South Adams, Massachusetts. In 1836 he moved to Utica, where he worked six months on the locks of the Chenango Canal, and the following year he moved to Holland Patent. He built a number of stone buildings in this area, but this house is his only cobblestone production. It is probably safe to credit this as the only Greek Revival house in America with cobblestone columns.

159

99. Montgomery County, Simms House, 5 Broad Street, Fultonville

Jephtha Simms, the original owner of this house, was a historian and author, particularly interested in Revolutionary history as well as that of the Mohawk Valley. Like Sir Walter Scott and James Fenimore Cooper, he preferred to live in a Gothic atmosphere. Simms gathered the water-rounded stones from the Mohawk and Schoharie valleys and had this house built in 1850. The wood wing at the right rear with the crenellated parapet was added in 1883.

100. ALBANY COUNTY, Receiving Vault, Guilderland Cemetery, Guilderland

The cobbles on the front wall are spaced a uniform distance apart so that the eye travels upward, from one stone to the next, on a diagonal. There is no emphasis given to the mortar joints, it would almost seem as if the mason pressed the stones into the wet mortar coat. This treatment is typical of several cobblestone buildings in Albany County. The stone tablet over the door has the date 1872.

101. MONROE COUNTY, House Fragment (now demolished), Sheldon Road, Mendon Township

COBBLESTONE LANDMARKS OF NEW YORK STATE

was composed in twelve-point Linotype Bodoni Book and leaded one point, with display type in Bodoni Ultra-bold, printed offset on 80-pound Warren's Lustro Offset Enamel Dull, Smyth-sewn and bound over boards in Columbia Bayside Vellum, and also adhesive bound with paper covers tipped on by Maple-Vail Book Manufacturing Group, Inc., and published by

SYRACUSE UNIVERSITY PRESS